Egg Art

Claude Nassiet

Illustrations
by
Marc BERTHIER

Photos PROMOPHOT

DRAKE PUBLISHERS INC. NEW YORK

introduction

Eggs have a beautiful form which is very pleasant to the touch, a form which has often inspired artists to decorate them directly or to reproduce them in rich, smooth materials.

People have always enjoyed offering eggs as gifts and, whether painted or decorated with various materials, these eggs are often very beautiful and precious objects. Today we invite you, young and old, to join us in this work.

Handling an empty eggshell provides an especially good occasion to teach youngsters how to work with a delicate, fragile object, and to thereby acquire a certain sensitivity to touch, as well as a steady hand.

The suggestions for decoration and transformation which we have included here are all relatively simple and demand only a little care and patience. The complimentary materials are all those that can be found at home, in schools or in hobby and handicraft centers. If you don't have the exact same materials as specified here it is usually possible to find a replacement... also a good occasion to personalize your work even more.

We have intentionally omitted here the simple painting and coloring of eggs, as this type of decorating is quite common and we prefer to offer you more original ideas.

For certain objects we have also chosen to use plaster "decoy" eggs, such as those placed in hen-houses to encourage the hens to lay. Of course you can always make your own plaster eggs by filling an eggshell (explained below), but the ready-made egg is sometimes preferable in order to avoid too much preparation time when working with children. The low price of such plaster eggs easily permits their usage in these cases. You can find plaster eggs in poultry-supply stores and in the pet sections of certain large department stores.

Besides the many ideas for decorating eggs which you will find here, we have also included some suggestions for creating interesting and amusing articles from egg cartons. These modern packages offer various shapes which can be fun to transform into practical objects. We sincerely hope that these few ideas will lead to many, many more ideas of your own.

practical hints

HOW TO EMPTY AN EGG:

• Use a needle to pierce a tiny hole at the top of the pointed end of the egg.

• Make a second hole at the other end of the egg and gradually enlarge it.

• Blow into the top hole in order to force the yolk and white of the egg out of the bottom hole. Retain the contents of the egg for cooking.

• Carefully wash the inside of the empty shell by running water through the holes several times.

Note that each time we refer to an egg in the following pages we shall be referring to an egg emptied in this manner.

It is, of course, possible to decorate hard-boiled eggs. This eliminates the necessity of emptying them, and they are much easier to work with than empty shells. However, besides the obvious waste involved (and it is a shame to waste good eggs !), hard-boiled eggs eventually turn rotten and emit a very unpleasant odor.

HOW TO CUT AN EGG

• After emptying the egg, enlarge the top hole by using a cuticle scissors with curved blades.

• Gently cut the shell to the desired height.

• Be careful - the sides are crumbly and fragile. Reinforce them by pouring a little liquid plaster along the inside or by varnishing them with ordinary clear nail polish.

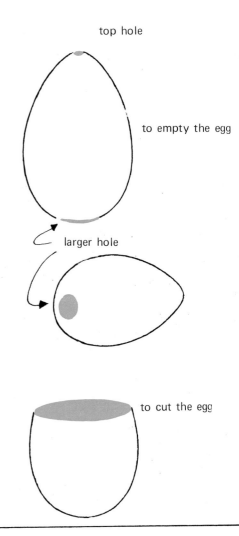

top hole

to empty the egg

larger hole

to cut the egg

5

HOW TO FILL AN EGG WITH PLASTER

• Prepare the plaster: Put a little water in a glass or plastic container and pour modeling plaster or plaster of paris into it. Beat the mixture with a spoon until the plaster reaches the consistency of "pancake" batter; the plaster must be liquid enough to pass through the larger hole of the egg.

• Plug the smaller hole with your finger or with a piece of Scotch tape. Moisten the interior of the egg by running a little water into it and turning it over a few times. Empty the excess water.

• Since it is rather difficult to fill an egg with plaster through such a tiny opening, you can simplify matters by making a tiny aluminium-foil funnel (fashion a foil cone and clip the tip). Insert this funnel into the larger hole of the egg and place the egg itself in an egg-cup or in a carton so that it rests upright.

• Carefully fill the egg with plaster. If you prefer to make a solid plaster egg, fill the egg completely and, once the plaster has dried, crack the shell to remove the egg. If, however, you simply wish to strengthen the egg, fill the shell only partially, since plaster expands slightly in drying and will easily cause the egg to crack.

• Wipe up immediately any drops of plaster which may have splashed.

• Allow the plaster to dry completely before proceeding with the decoration of the egg.

HOW TO REINFORCE AN EGG

It is often advisable to weight the eggs or to reinforce the shell with a plaster lining. To do so:

• Pour a little liquid plaster into the egg.

• Wait a few minutes until it begins to harden, then turn the egg slowly until all sides are well-coated.

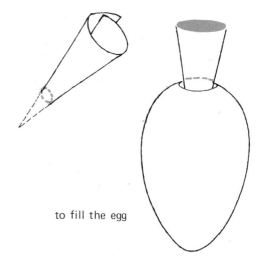

to fill the egg

to reinforce the egg

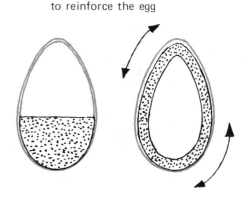

DECORATION

with beads

MATERIAL

- An egg reinforced with plaster.
- A sheet of paper.
- Various colored beads.
- Glue.
- A wooden matchstick.

PROCEDURE

- Glue a tiny square of paper over the holes of the egg.
- Spread out the beads on a sheet of paper, freely mixing the various colored beads.
- Put a good coating of glue on a small surface of the egg.
- Role the egg in the beads, which adhere to the glued surface.

Use a wooden matchstick to remove those beads which are not well glued.

- Wait a short time for the glue to dry completely.
- Repeat the process, gluing the adjacent surface to the area already covered with beads and so on until the egg is entirely decorated with beads.

SOME REMARKS

This type of decorating is extremely simple and the result is gratifying.

You can decorate an egg with beads of only one color if you prefer. If you do use several colors, avoid using more than three or four at one time.

Several eggs decorated in this manner and placed in a tiny basket or bowl make an impressive centerpiece.

8

with wool

MATERIAL

- An egg.
- Glue.
- Scraps of wool, preferably wide and of different colors.
- A pencil, a wooden matchstick.

PROCEDURE

- Using your pencil, mark on the eggs the lines of separation for the different bands of color. These will serve as guidelines for winding the wool.
- Begin in the middle of the egg, at the widest point, and make a strip of glue about two inches long. Apply the first piece of wool and press it down with your finger so that it adheres well.
- Add more glue and continue the process, winding the wool tightly around the egg.
- To change the color, cut the piece of wool at the same height as the one with which you began the band and continue the winding process with the next color.
- Continue winding the wool around the egg until half of it is covered.
- Finish at the end of the egg by cutting the wool arranging the last piece with your fingers as shown in the sketch.
- Now cover the other half of the egg in the same way.

SOME ADVICE

The wool must be wound very tightly. Use a matchstick to firmly pack each layer against the preceding ones.
These eggs are very light and can be easily mounted on a mobile. Just set aside a piece of wool which you have used to wind one of the ends and use it later to suspend the egg.

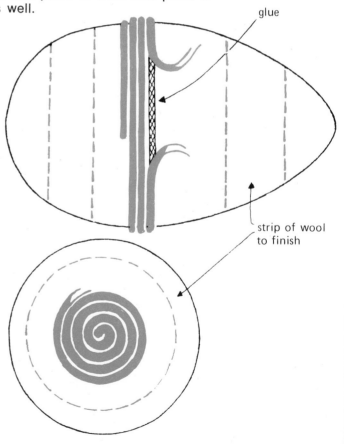

glue

strip of wool to finish

with color-coated candies

MATERIAL

- A plaster egg (this type of decorating material is rather heavy).
- Glue.
- Color-coated candies for example « Good and Plenty » or « Mem ».
- A pair of small tweezers.

PROCEDURE

- Spread a thick coat of glue over the widest part of the egg.
- Affix the candies to the egg with your fingers or a pair of small tweezers.
- Continue the process in this manner, turning the egg and gluing until you have covered the entire surface with the candies.

Be careful not to turn the candies in the glue when affixing them, since this will remove their shiny coating. Try to place them as directly as possible.

with sequins

MATERIAL

- An egg.
- Glue.
- Sequins.
- Silver-coated candies or decorative trim.
- A wooden matchstick.

PROCEDURE

- Using the materials at your disposal, first glue on the decorative trim or the candies. The trim is easy to manipulate and attach to the egg... and you can create any number of patterns with the candies.
- Once you have affixed the trim or the candies, fill in the uncovered surface with sequins. Spread glue over a small patch of the egg and affix the sequins one by one, using a moist matchstick to set them exactly in place.
- The sequins should slightly overlap one another like fish scales in order to avoid any gaps.

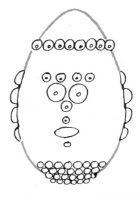

The final result is a collection of decorated eggs looking especially quaint and old-fashioned.

with sea shells

MATERIAL

- Preferably a plaster egg.
- Glue.
- A pair of tweezers.
- Some sand or colored powder.
- Some sea shells.

PROCEDURE

- Sort the shells according to shape and size.
- Begin gluing them to the two ends of the egg, trying to harmonize the colors and the shapes. Make sure that you have spread a good coating of glue over the surface of the egg; then use a pair of tweezers to affix the shells.
- You can decorate the egg completely in this manner or reserve some empty spaces where you may later want to glue sand, colored powders, a larger or more interesting shell, etc.

You can also make a very original picture frame by gluing a small photograph on one side of the egg and encircling it with sea shells.

sand

sea shells

with uncooked noodles

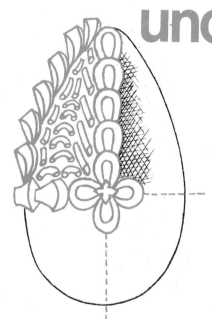

MATERIAL

- A plaster egg.
- Glue.
- A pair of tweezers.
- Small noodles or macaroni of various sizes and shapes.

PROCEDURE

- Glue on the largest noodles first, sticking them all around the egg horizontally and vertically (see sketch here opposite).
- Glue on those noodles which form the central motif.
- Coat a section of the uncovered background surface with a generous amount of glue and, using the tweezers, cover it with the smaller noodles. Fill in the rest of the egg in the same manner.

As you will also discover to be true in decorating with seeds, you can create any number of interesting motifs by using noodles of different sizes.

with seeds

modeling clay.

MATERIAL

- An egg.
- Glue.
- Tweezers.
- A good variety of seeds. Buy them in a pet store, if possible, and ask for an assortment for pigeons. You can also use rice and other dried vegetables like beans, lentils, split peas, kidney beans, etc.

PROCEDURE

TO DECORATE IN STRIPS

- Beginning at the widest part of the egg, coat the surface well with glue and put two or three seeds in place, holding them for a few seconds so that they adhere well to the egg.
- When you have finished gluing on one strip of seeds in this manner, continue with another type of seed.
- Use the smallest seeds to cover the two extremities.

TO DECORATE IN PATTERNS

- Cover the middle of the egg with glue and group four seeds together at the center, holding them in position for a few moments. Glue other seeds lengthwise around this grouping; then add some tiny split peas to the tips of the "flower".
- When everything has dried, turn the egg over and repeat the same pattern on the opposite side.

We have used uncooked rice to fill in the uncovered backround of the motif. To do so, put some glue on a small portion of this backround, scatter some rice over it. Then arrange the grains with tweezers. Repeat the process until the egg is well covered.

OTHER IDEAS:

If you put a ring of seeds around the bottom of the egg it will stand upright. A smaller ring around the top serves as a candle-holder.

If the eggs are wobbly, you can make a base out of a thick round piece of modeling clay.

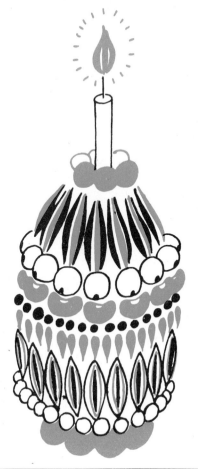

with mosaics

MATERIAL

- A plaster egg.
- Glue.
- Small glass mosaics.
- Tweezers.

PROCEDURE

- Begin at the widest part of the egg.
- Spread the glue over the middle area and pose the tiny squares with the aid of tweezers. Arrange them as evenly as possible since the effect is much more attractive.
- When you reach the ends, spread the mosaics out a bit so that you can go completely around the egg.

OTHER IDEAS

The pattern can be varied: strips of different colors, or simple patterns such as "cross-stitching". But avoid using too many colors so as not to give a haphazard impression.

You may also want to try mixing mosaics and beads (see photo page 12).

- Form the central motif by first gluing on the mosaics.
- Then fill in the backround in the following manner: make a paper funnel and fill it with beads. Cover a small surface of the background with glue and drop the beads onto the glued area; then arrange them more evenly with a matchstick.

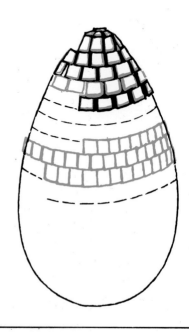

DECORATIVE OBJECTS
the flower

MATCH HOLDER

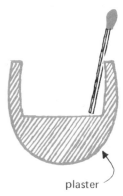

plaster

MATERIAL

- An egg.
- A piece of lightweight cardboard or pasteboard.
- Glue.
- Different colored pieces of felt.
- A piece of black friction paper (i.e. removed from a large box of kitchen matches).

friction surface

PROCEDURE

- Cut an eggshell in half and reinforce the bottom half by pouring plaster on the bottom and along the wells of the shell. The shell should be about half-filled with plaster.

- To make the base, use a strip of cardboard seven inches long by 1½ inches high. Form a cylinder of the same diameter as the egg and then glue the ends of the cardboard strip together.

- Around the outside of the cylinder, glue a strip of one-inch wide friction paper.

- Glue the inside of the cylinder completely in order to hold the egg firmly in place.

- Following the patterns given below cut out five felt petals for **A**, five for **B** and five for **C**.

- Attach petals A first, all around the top of the shell. Then glue on petals B and C alternately, arranging them in the same way as shown in the sketch opposite. Petals C should be attached just above the friction paper. In this manner they are glued to both the cardboard cylinder and to the egg, thereby reinforcing the whole thing.

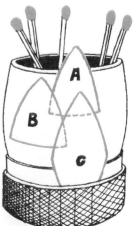

Put some matches into the shell; and the sulfur tips form the stamen of the flower.

And there you have an easy-to-make and attractive gift!

A   **B**   **C**

baby chicks

MATERIAL

For each chick:
- An egg.
- Light yellow-colored cotton-balls.
- Glue.
- A small wire.
- A bit of yellow felt.
- Gold-colored yarn.
- Two beads, or two black mosaics, or two black snaps for the eyes.
- Some lightweight cardboard.

PROCEDURE

- Cut the beak (shown below) from the cardboard and glue it on the egg. Cover the beak with yarn or with two small pieces of felt cut out of the same pattern.
- Make the chick's leg by bending the wire into the form indicated here. Wind yarn around part of it as in photo, page 21. Insert the top of the leg into the hole at the bottom of the egg, the one which you used to empty it.
- Coat the egg generously with glue and cover it with the cotton. Make sure that the area around the wire base is well glued by stuffing some of cotton into the bottom hole of the egg.
- Add more cotton in the appropriate place for the tail.
- Finish by gluing on either the snaps or the mosaics which you have chosen for the eyes.

c

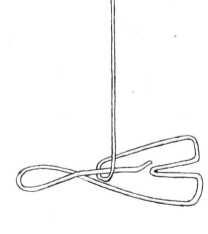

A

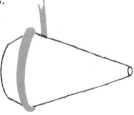

B

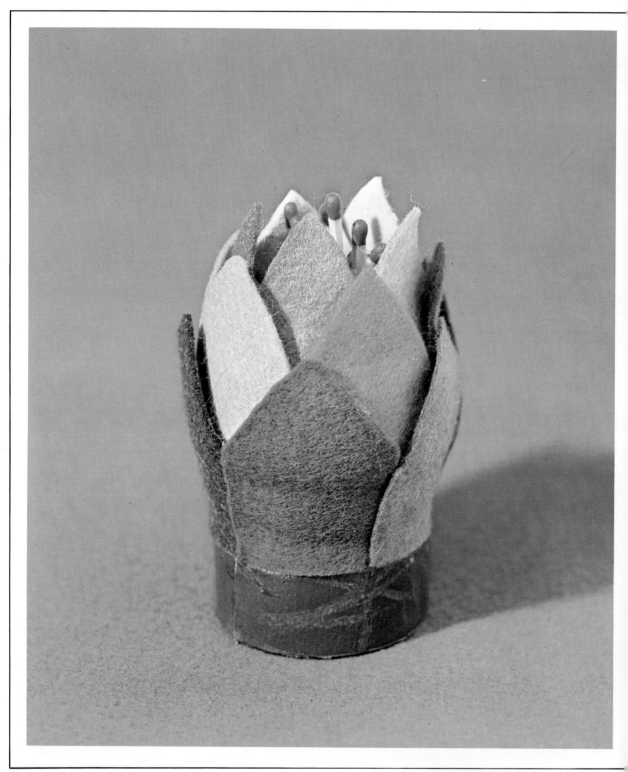

with broken eggshells

- Broken eggshells of different shades (you can use the shells from hard-boiled eggs).
- Colored powder
- Glue.
- Some sheets of white paper.
- A wooden matchstick.
- An object to decorate: a glass jar, a lampshade, a glass, a pot, a flask, etc.

PROCEDURE

- Arrange the small heaps of colored powder on the sheets of paper (one color on each sheet).
- Prepare the pieces of shells by being sure to remove the thin white inner skin.
- Coat the object to be decorated with a good layer of glue, covering not more than $1/2$ square inch of the surface at one time. Put the first piece of shell into place and press it firmly until it shatters into tiny, irregular pieces.
- Sprinkle the area immediately with colored powder and shake over a sheet of paper in order to recover the powder which has not adhered to the sticky surfaces.
- Continue the process, remembering to vary the shades of the shells.

SOME ADDITIONAL SUGGESTIONS

Don't use too many colored powders... two or three are sufficient.

By cleverly arranging the different shades of shells you can obtain a design which is almost regular and very attractive. The already very delicate effect of this type of decoration can be heightened if the object is transparent. This idea is therefore particularly suitable for decorating glasses which contain scented candles.

Lacking such, you can get the same effect by attaching an ordinary candle to the bottom of the glass or jar, provided the container is solid enough to withstand the heat.

a bird on a branch

PROCEDURE

• Cut out a cardboard pyramid for the base; fold and glue it.

• To make the bird, begin by winding the yarn on one side of the egg to form a wing (wind in the same direction as indicated in the sketch opposite). Do the same on the opposite side for the other wing.

• Cut out a small triangle of cardboard, wind yarn around it and glue it into place for the beak.

• Then, starting from one of the wings, wind a different color yarn around the egg to represent the bird's body. When you reach the middle of the egg, fashion a tail with several pieces of yarn placed under the yarn that you are winding around the egg. This will hold the "tail-feathers" securely in place. Make sure that these pieces are long enough to later be clipped to the desired length.

• Insert the wire into the bottom hole of the egg. Do this at the same moment that you wind the yarn around this portion of the egg, so that the wire is held in place in the same manner that the "tail-feathers" are.

• Place the other end of the wire into the top of the base. Then wind yarn around both the wire and the base in order to strengthen the whole assemblage.

• Glue on the snaps for the eyes.

OTHER IDEAS

One or several of these birds can be perched on a few branches placed in a vase or flowerpot. Use the wire to attach them to the branches.

You can transform this bird into a paperweight by making a heavier base. One possibility is to stick the wire into a base made of heavy modeling clay. Another suggestion is to pour plaster into an empty container and, before the plaster is completely dry, insert the wire supporting the bird. Once the base has dried (after being removed from the mold), paint and varnish it.

MATERIAL

• An egg.
• Pieces of leftover yarn.
• Glue.
• Lightweight cardboard.
• A small piece of wire.
• Two snaps.

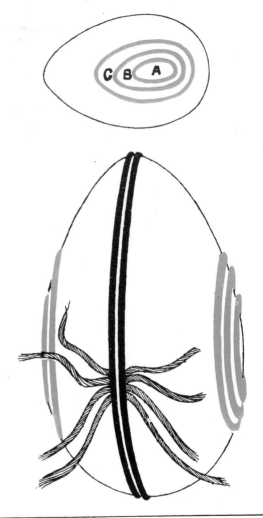

fire balloons

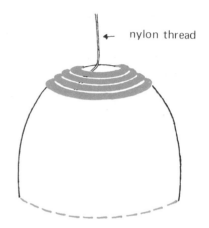

MATERIAL

- Two eggs.
- Scraps of yarn.
- Two walnut shells.
- Nylon thread, as used in window displays (1).
- Aluminium foil.
- Three pieces of wire: one 10 inches long, another 14 inches long, and the last 4 inches long.
- Glue.

PROCEDURE

- Wind the yarn around the eggs according to the directions given on page 10, remembering to begin at the middle. Continue winding towards the larger end of the egg.
- When you reach the top glue a piece of nylon thread under the last evolution of yarn. This will later be used to suspend the "balloon".
- Cover the other half of the egg in the same manner, again beginning at the middle and working toward the smaller end of the egg. Place three additional pieces of yarn on each side of the egg (under the wound yarn) to which you will later attach the "gondola".
- Each "gondola" is made of a walnut shell. Glue the pieces of yarn (which are hanging from the egg) to the inside of the walnut shells; then cover the shells with aluminium foil. You can decorate them further by gluing one or two strips of yarn to their sides.
- A silver-foil "sun", tops off the mobile. Insert

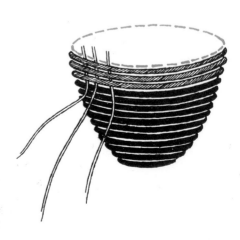

(1) Found in the notions department of most large stores or in hardware stores.

26

the 10-inch wire into one side of the ball of foil, and the 4-inch wire into the other side.

• Connect the two wires with a piece of wool knotted at each corner (see sketch).

MOUNTING THE MOBILES

• Attach the two balloons to the wire by their nylon threads (**A**, **B** on the sketch).

• Attach this first wire to the second wire, **C**, **D**.

• Attach another nylon thread, **E**, which will be used to hang the mobile.

• Slide the knots of the different points of attachment along the wires until you find the exact equilibrium of the mobile. This will depend on the weight of the eggs and of the yarn used, as well as on the size of the "sun". When you have found the equilibrium, glue the knots to the wire.

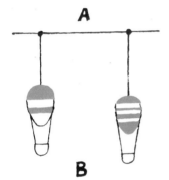

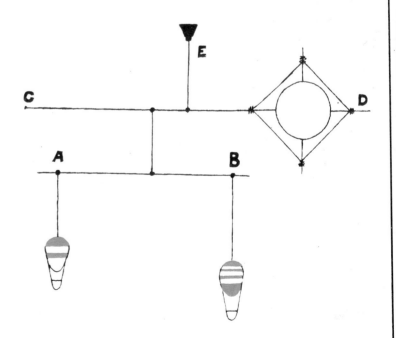

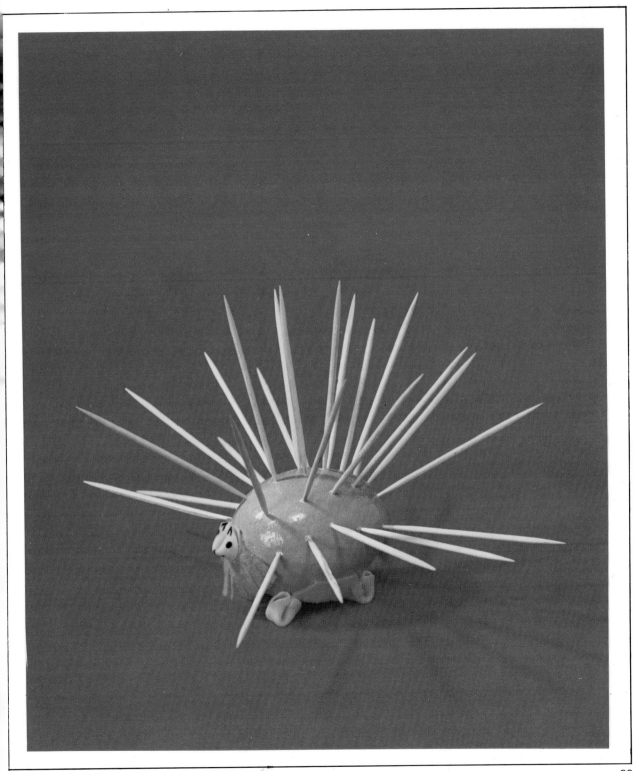

the pricking porcupine

HOLDS TOOTHPICKS OR OLIVE-PICKS

MATERIAL

- A plaster-filled egg.
- A long darning needle.
- Some pieces of felt.
- A few uncooked noodles.
- Glue.
- Clear varnish.
- A felt-tipped pen.
- Toothpicks or olive-picks.

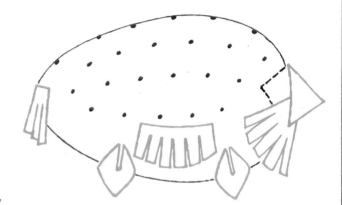

PROCEDURE

- Using the darning needle, carefully pierce holes in one side of the egg. Turn the needle in the holes until they are big enough to accomodate the toothpicks or olive-picks. Leave enough space between the holes so that the shell will not crack.
- Varnish the egg.
- Glue on the four feet and the head. Make the head by inserting part of the noodle into the larger hole in the egg.
- Draw in the eyes and the mouth with a felt-tipped pen.
- Cut out the felt tail, the two sides and the collar according to the patterns provided here.
- All that remains is to stick the toothpicks or olive-picks into the holes.

This tiny porcupine takes only a few minutes to make, but it can add so much to your set table or buffet. Just remember: pierce the holes carefully.

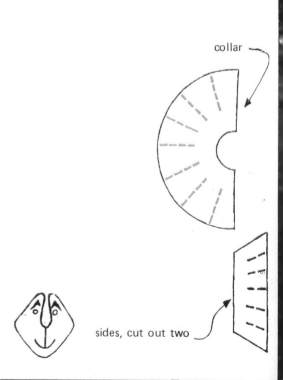

collar

tail →

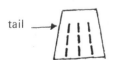

sides, cut out two

turtles

KNIFE-HOLDERS OR PLACE-MARKERS

For each turtle:
- A plaster-filled egg.
- Some uncooked noodles.
- Glue.
- Colored felt-tipped pens.
- Clear varnish.

PROCEDURE

- Glue on the four noodles for the feet. Add the head, which is composed of two noodles glued on top of each other (see sketch). The neck portion is slightly pushed into the hole through which the egg was filled with plaster.
- Decorate the eggs by covering them with colorful scales (use the felt-tipped pens).
- Varnish

OTHER IDEAS

These turtles, so quick and easy to make, are amusing knife-holders or place-markers. For the latter, just write the names of your table guests on the turtles' backs.

Another idea is to glue an average sized candle to the back of each turtle and light up a celebration table with a series of tiny turtles.

the snail

- An egg.
- Leftover pieces of yarn.
- Glue.
- Small pieces of lightweight cardboard.
- Two wooden matchsticks.
- A large needle.

PROCEDURE

- Begin on one side of the egg at the widest part. Cover the egg completely with the various pieces of wool, winding in the direction indicated on the sketch (here opposite).
- Cut form **C** out of lightweight cardboard and wind the yarn tightly around it.
- Cover the two matchsticks with wool.
- Pierce the cardboard with the large needle at the indicated points and insert the matchsticks into these holes to create the horns.
- Bend the cardboard piece slightly upwards at the front end to suggest the raised head of the snail. Glue the egg to the rear portion.

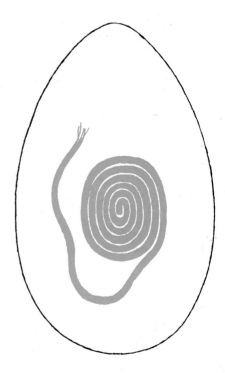

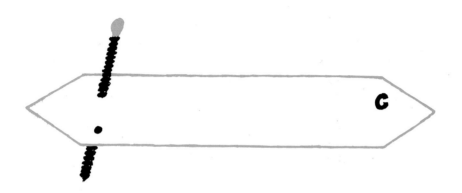

auntie mary

MENU-HOLDER

MATERIAL

- An egg.
- Glue.
- A portion of a cardboard cylinder (1), or some lightweight cardboard or pasteboard.
- Leftover pieces of wool (for the hair).
- Black felt-tipped pen.
- Colored paper for the clothing or, better yet, magazine clippings.
- White paper.
- Scissors.

PROCEDURE

THE BODY:

- Make a cylinder 6 inches long by 2 inches in diameter, either by cutting one to the right dimensions with a serrated knife or by rolling a piece of lightweight cardboard into a cylinder (see sketch).
- Clip notches of $^1/_2$ inch each around the top of the cylinder and squeeze them together until you have an opening corresponding to the size of the egg which will form the head.

"Dress" the cylinder in colored paper and turn the paper in at both ends for a much neater effect.

- Decorate according to your fancy, adding the arms as you do so.
- Cut out the collar, apron, etc. and add them to the finished "body".

(1) Cardboard cylinders such as those holding adhesive paper, paper-towels, etc. You can probably find discarded ones at the grocery store.

saw along the dotted lines

THE HEAD

• Make the hair by gluing the wool onto the crown of the egg head. Wind the "hair" into a little bun and glue it to the very top. Now draw on the face with the felt-tipped pen.

• Put a good coating of glue around inside of the top of the cylinder, then insert the egg. This should firmly attach the head to the body.

• Write the menu on a strip of white paper. Glue it to the body or slide it into a slot made with the serrated knife. Roll the menu inwards.

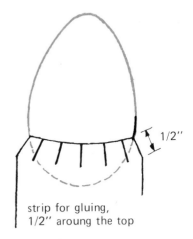

1/2"

strip for gluing, 1/2" aroung the top

strip for gluing, 1" at the top and bottom to be notched and glued.

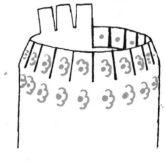

1/2", for gluing

5"

8"

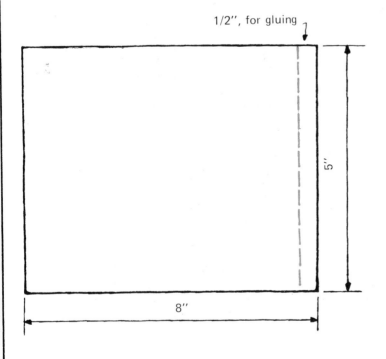

miss flower hat

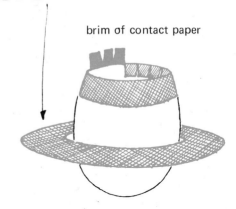

brim of contact paper

MATERIAL

- An egg reinforced with plaster.
- A cardboard cylinder or some lightweight cardboard with which to make one.
- Magazine clippings.
- Some pasteboard.
- Contact paper in a straw pattern or the color of light wood.
- Glue.
- Decorative trim.
- Clear varnish.
- Pink and black felt-tipped pens.

PROCEDURE

THE BODY:

- Follow the directions for Auntie Mary, page 34.
- The clothes and the accessories are made of clipped magazine photos.

THE HEAD AND THE HAT:

- Cut off the larger end of an egg and reinforce the bottom and the walls of the egg with plaster.
- Draw on the face and the hair, color the cheeks.
- Strengthen the shell by varnishing it.
- Cut out a cardboard hat brim — the diameter around the outside of the brim should be about 4 inches, and the diameter of the inner hole should be about 2 inches, depending upon the size of the egg.
- Work the brim up from the lower part of the face to the edge of the contact paper band at the top of the egg. Conceal the line of transition with a strip of decorative trim

strip of contact paper, notched and tucked in.

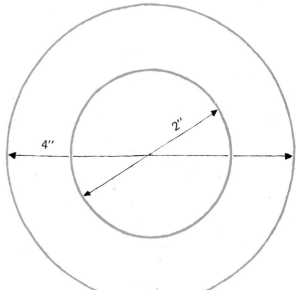

glued around the egg and tied in back like a hat-band.

- Attach the head to the body as for Auntie Mary.
- Place a piece of damp absorbent cotton inside and plant lentils, soybeans, etc.

egg candle

MATERIAL

- An egg.
- Remnants of ordinary white candles.
- Colored pencils or crayons.
- Salvaged bits of cotton material.
- An old saucepan.
- A source of heat to melt the candles.

PROCEDURE

- First prepare the candle wick, which is made either by using a real wick from a candle which you have melted, or by rolling scraps of old cotton material together. Make the wick a bit longer than the height of the egg.
- Pass the wick through the holes which you used to empty the egg.
- Fold down the pieces extending at either end and attach them to the egg with Scotch tape. The wick must be taut on the inside of the egg.
- Melt the pieces of candles in the saucepan and then pour the wax into the egg through the hole.
- To color the wax, scrape some of the colored crayons or colored pencils into the saucepan with the candles to be melted.
- To make a rainbow candle of several colors, just change the color of the crayons which you melt into the wax and pour each successive color into the egg. But be sure to allow the previous color to dry before adding the next one.
- When the egg is full, let it cool and then remove the Scotch-tape holding down the wick ends. Break the shell by tapping it very lightly. If the thin white skin of the shell adheres to the candle, rub lightly with your finger to remove it.
- Straighten the wick at the top and cut it at the bottom along the wax-line.
- Melt the base a little so that the candle can be set upright.

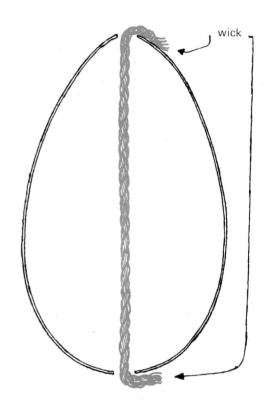

wick

floating eggs

MATERIAL

- Several eggs.
- Pieces of candles.
- Colored pencils or crayons.
- Salvaged pieces of old cotton material.
- An old saucepan and a heat source to melt the candles.
- Matches.

PROCEDURE

For each egg:

- Cut off the top of the egg and prepare a wick as for the egg candles on page 38.
- Place the wick in the egg, centering it as much as possible. Use a few drops of candle wax to fasten the wick to the bottom of the egg. Roll the unattached end of the wick around a matchstick and place the matchstick across the top opening of the egg. This will hold the wick taut.
- Pour the wax into the egg, filling it only three-quarters full. When the wax has cooled, cut the wick at about $1/2$ inch above the wax. Place the eggs in a glass or metal bowl which has been half-filled with water and light the wicks. The effect is enchanting.

SOME ADVICE

For an even more beautiful effect, try to use different shades of lighter or darker eggshells.

You can also color the wax, as for the egg candles. If you place the bowl on a mirror or in front of one, the effect will be even more breathtaking.

Why not replace the traditional birthday candles with these floating candles?... But if you've passed your 7th birthday you'll need a lot of breath to blow them all out.

wax →

geisha girl

This charming little Japanese lady bows and shakes her head at the slightest touch.

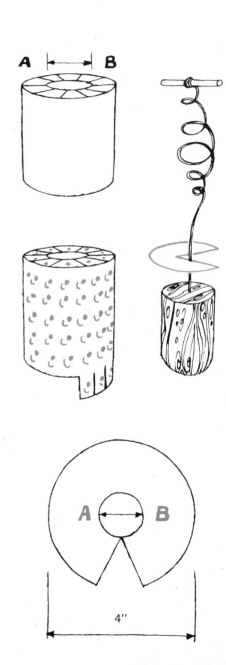

MATERIAL

- An egg.
- Plaster.
- A cylinder (or cardboard with which to make one).
- Lightweight cardboard.
- An old spring from a retractable ball-point pen.
- A wooden matchstick.
- A cork.
- Glue.
- Colored papers for decorating the cylinder.
- Colored felt-tipped pens.

PROCEDURE

THE BODY

- Cut or make a cylinder 4 inches high. Clip notches of 1/2 inch each around the top of the cylinder, then fold them in very evenly, as if you were making a bottom (see sketch). The central opening **A B** should correspond to the diameter of the cork which you are using. Make any necessary adjustments.
- Dress and decorate the cylinder as you like.
- Cut the collar out of lightweight cardboard. The opening **A B** of the collar should also correspond to the diameter of the cork. Glue colored paper on the top side of the collar and then glue it on the cylinder. Be sure that the two openings **A B** are exactly superimposed.

THE HEAD:

- Cut off the small end of an egg. Draw on the face and the hair with the felt-tipped pens, then varnish.
- Unwind the spring and implant one end of it in the center of the cork.

- Glue a piece of paper with a slit in it to the top of the cork. The slit will allow for passage of the wire spring.
- Wind the other end of the spring around a small piece of a wooden matchstick.
- The neck is made from a band of paper which is glued around the top of the cork. This paper should be about 1 inch high and of the same color as the collar.
- Turn the egg head over and pour some plaster into the bottom quarter of it. While the plaster is still wet, embed the matchstick and its attached spring into it.
- When the plaster has dried, stick the cork into the top opening of the cylinder. By tipping the cork slightly, you should obtain a head which is quite straight in relation to the body, but which shakes at the slightest touch.

This amusing knickknack is easy to make, the only delicate step being the attachment of the head... but the effort is well rewarded.

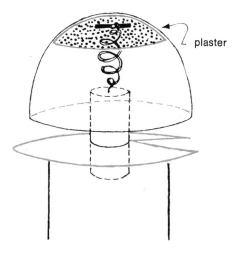

plaster

mama and her twins

MATERIAL

- Two balls of styrofoam.
- Some leftover bits of wallpaper.

PROCEDURE

THE MAMA:

- Make the body in the same way as for Auntie Mary (page 34), and dress her with scraps of wallpaper.

THE CHILDREN:

- The body of each twin is made of a cardboard cylinder.
- Dress the cylinders with wallpaper and glue a styrofoam head on top.
- Glue the twins on each side of their mother.

Using this same principle for other characters, this idea might be helpful for making a new Christmas Nativity scene.

masks

- A plastic egg carton (holding six eggs).
- Cuticle scissors.
- Glue.
- Absorbent cotton.
- Pieces of yarn.
- A large needle.
- A piece of elastic or a rubber band.

PROCEDURE

THE MUSTACHE MASK:

- Cut out a section of the egg carton comprising two concave egg cups and one separation dome.
- Using cuticle scissors, cut off the bottom half of each of the two egg cups. Then slit two holes in the base of the dome to create a nose.
- Twist some yarn and glue it above the eyeholes to simulate the bushy eyebrows.
- Sew ringlets of yarn under the tip of the nose.
- Glue a rubber band or piece of elastic to the sides to hold the mask in place.

THE WHITE MASK:

- Cut the same form as above out of the plastic carton. After you have cut off the bottom halves of the two egg cups, slit a hole in the base of each one and set them, inversed, into the eyeholes of the mask (see photo page 48). Hold them in place by spreading glue around the inside of the concave egg cups.

Glue the cotton around the outside of the mask and around the nose to simulate the hair and mustache.

the clown

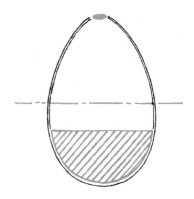

MATERIAL

- An egg.
- A small styrofoam ball.
- Some white drawing paper.
- A yellow cotton-ball.
- Felt-tipped pens.
- Decorative trim or pieces of yarn.
- Two wires, each about 10 inches long.
- Nylon thread.
- Glue.
- A large needle.

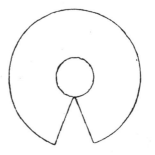

PROCEDURE

- Fill an egg one-third full of plaster, to weight the base.
- Decorate the body. Here we have fashioned a pair of overalls made of trim glued on the egg. You can substitute yarn if you prefer.
- Cut out the feet, arms and collar and glue them in place.
- Using a large needle, make a small hole on each side of the body and pass one of the wires through the arms and the body (see photo).

- The head is made of styrofoam and the face drawn on with felt-tipped pens. Use the yellow cotton-ball for the hair.
- Tie the clown to the second wire with the nylon thread, then glue the knots in place.

By shaking the top wire, the clown swings and even turns a full somersault.

You can also make a mobile by tying a nylon thread to the middle of the top wire.

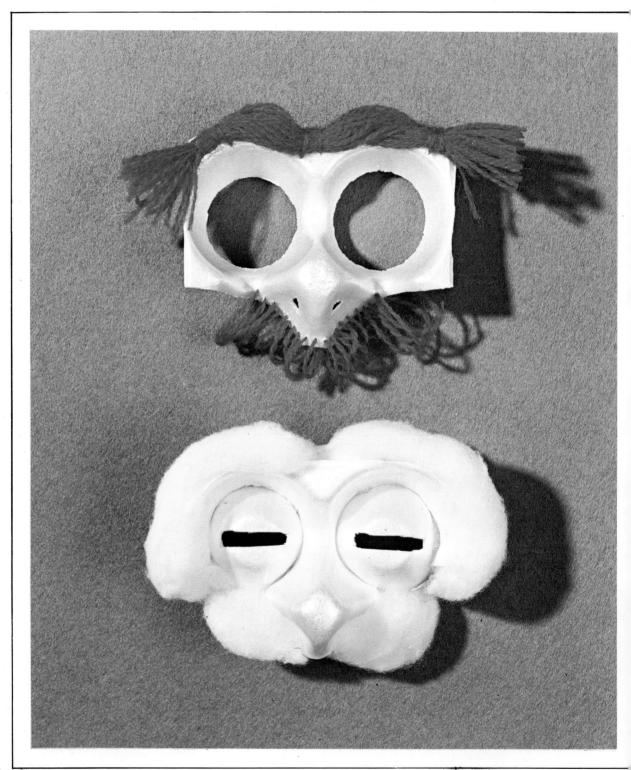

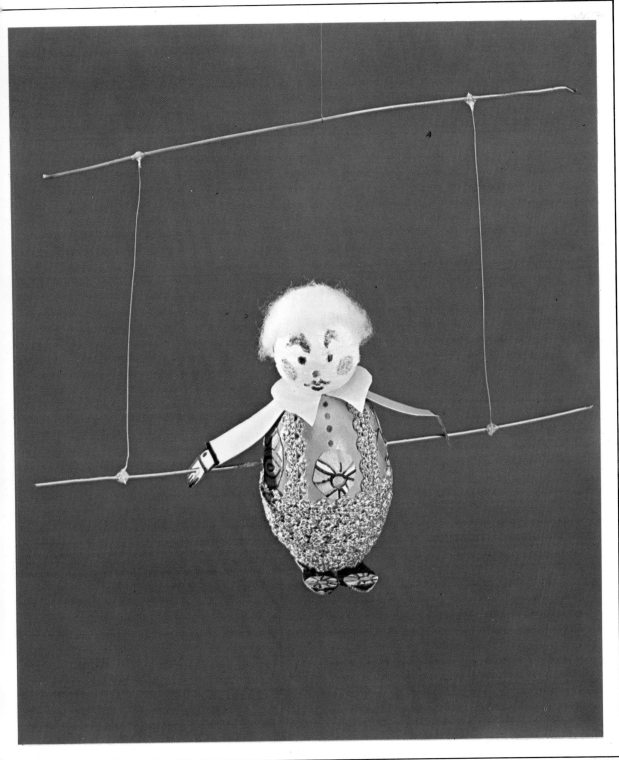

the polite knight

A very polite knight, indeed, since he nods his head at the slightest draft.

MATERIAL

- An egg.
- Aluminum-foil.
- Lightweight cardboard or pasteboard.
- Some feathers.
- An aluminum tube (½ inch long).
- A small saw for cutting metal (a hacksaw).
- Some modeling clay.
- A piece of wire.
- Glue.
- Some felt or colored paper.

PROCEDURE

THE BODY:

- Make the cylinder out of a rectangular piece of cardboard, 5 inches by 8 inches.

THE HEAD:

- Draw the facial traits on the egg.
- Glue on the strips of aluminum foil to make the helmet.
- Insert the feather plumage into the top hole of the egg.

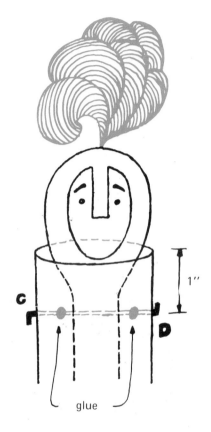

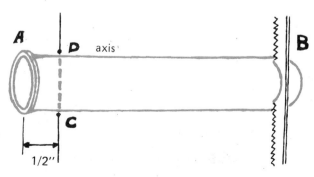

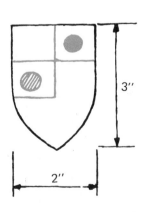

MOUNTING THE HEAD:

• Pierce two transverse holes in the aluminum tube, as illustrated in the sketch on page 50, and insert the wire axis through holes **C** and **D**.

• Glue on the strips of felt or heavy paper which attach the egg to the tube (use very heavy paper and plenty of glue). Cover these strips with foil.

• When the head stands straight, turn over the whole assemblage and, holding it by the axis (see sketch here opposite), insert modeling clay into the other end of the tube. When the weight of the clay is sufficient, the head will tilt back up and return to its normal position.

ATTACHING THE HEAD TO THE BODY:

• Pierce the cardboard body cylinder on each side at about 1 inch from the top. Insert the axis and turn up the ends. Put a drop of glue on each side of the metal tube which is inside of the cylinder, so that the head doesn't slip onto the wire.

• At the same time, gradually add more modeling clay to the base of the tube if the head does not shake easily enough. Add the clay little by little until a suitable weight is established.

• Cover the cylinder with aluminum-foil.

• Glue on the cardboard shield, which you have covered with colored paper or felt.

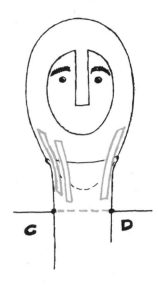

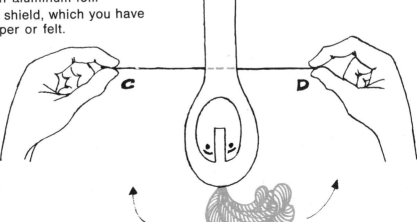

modeling clay

an original light-fixture

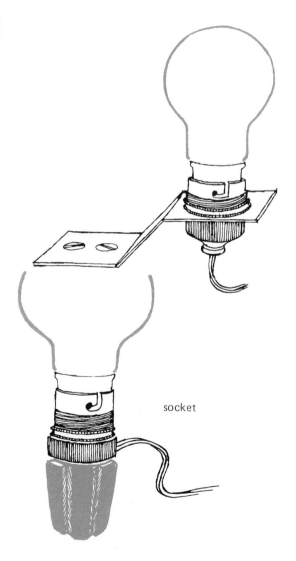

socket

MATERIAL

- Three large sheets of egg carton, the kind found in dairies. Make sure that these sheets are all the same size.
- Another piece of egg carton for cutting out the legs of the lamp.
- Three thumb-tacks.
- Glue.
- A square of plywood about 17 inches on each side.
- An electrical socket and its cord.

PROCEDURE

- Assemble the three sheets of egg carton into a triangle by gluing the inner corners of one sheet to the border of another. Let it dry.
- Place this triangular form on a large sheet of paper and mark out the exact location of the cartons.
- Using the sheet of paper as your reference, use a ruler to draw a triangular pattern, adding $1/4$ additional inch all around.
- Cut the sheet of plywood according to this pattern.
- The plywood can be tinted with Chinese ink or wood-stained, then waxed.
- Glue the socket into the center of this plywood base or, if necessary, use a screwdriver to attach a small metal brace with a hole in it to accomodate the socket (see sketch here opposite).
- Cut three cones out of the additional piece of egg carton, then glue them under the base to make the legs. To reinforce them, insert a tack into each one through the top of the base.

• Glue the assembled egg cartons onto the base. The electrical cord and plug are passed through one of the cut-out egg cups in the carton sides.

To give even more light, you can pierce some holes in the receding sections of the walls of the lamp. Use a scissor's tip to puncture the egg carton, then enlarge the holes by inserting a paint brush handle or a pencil into them from the exterior.

foot

the wheel of fish

MATERIAL

- Some eggs.
- Wire, or an old lamp shade frame.
- Glue.
- Scraps of felt or fabric samples.
- Nylon thread.
- A knitting needle.
- Scraps of yarn.

PROCEDURE

• Each egg becames a fish by your gluing various felt shapes to the sides of it (see photo page 57). Note that only sample pieces have been used to decorate these fish.

• Here and on page 56 you will find some sketches to assist you in decorating the eggs, but remember that "anything goes" for these eccentric fish.

• The fish are suspended by a piece of yarn passed through one of the felt decorations. Use the knitting needle to attach the yarn, then knot and glue underneath the felt piece, firmly fastening the whole thing to the egg.

MOUNTING THE MOBILE

• Make a wire circle. If your wire is too fine, double it and wind Scotch tape around it to maintain the shape.

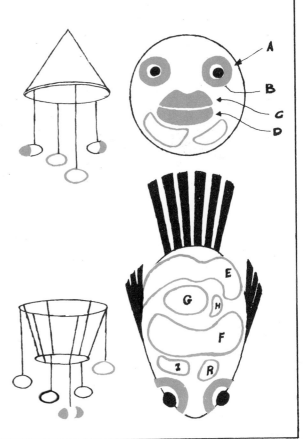

- Cover the circle with yarn.
- Attach a nylon thread to each side of the circle to suspend the mobile. Set the knots in place and glue.
- Suspend the fish with pieces of yarn which are wound around the wire circle until the equilibrium is established. (Some of them will be wound more or less than others, depending on their weight.) Glue the knots in place.

OTHER IDEAS

The fish alone make delightful Christmas tree decorations.

They can also be mounted on a mobile of another shape, such as the one for the Fire Balloons (page 27).

You can avoid making the wire circle by simply using an old lamp shade frame (see sketch page 55). Note that the larger circle is on top.

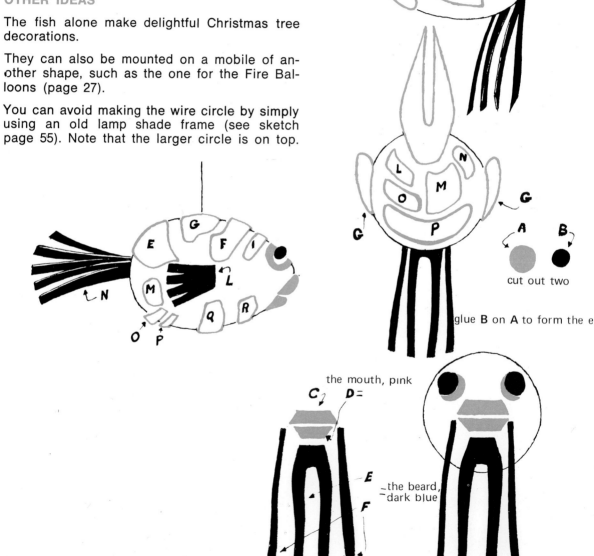

cut out two

glue **B** on **A** to form the eye

the mouth, pink

the beard,
dark blue

the flowered yardstick

Among the various cartons available, the most attractive are round ones. Both the shape and material lend themselves to numerous possibilities for decoration.

MATERIAL

- Half of a round carton.
- Felt-tipped pens.
- A tapemeasure.
- Some pieces of felt.

PROCEDURE

- Decorate the interior of the half-carton with your felt-tipped pens.
- Glue or tack the tapemeasure to the wall, the first number at the bottom. The tapemeasure becomes the stem of the flower.
- Glue the flower (the carton) to the top of the stem.
- Indicate the height of the child with a felt leaf tacked to the stem of the flower. If there also several children in the family you may want to use a different colored leaf for each child.
- On the reverse side of each leaf you can also glue a sticker indicating the date that the child was last measured.

There is only one inconvenience to this imaginative and easy-to-make yardstick: the numbers on the tapemeasure will be upside-down. To remedy this, all you need is enough patience to trace the inches and corresponding numbers on a wooden slat and substitute the slat for the cloth tapemeasure.

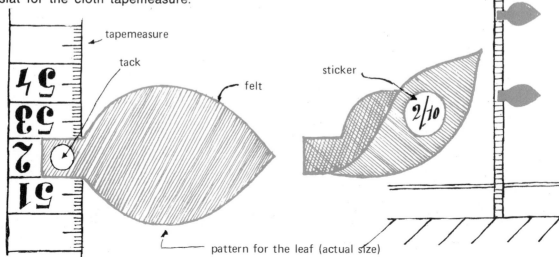

tapemeasure

tack

felt

sticker

pattern for the leaf (actual size)

a modern lamp

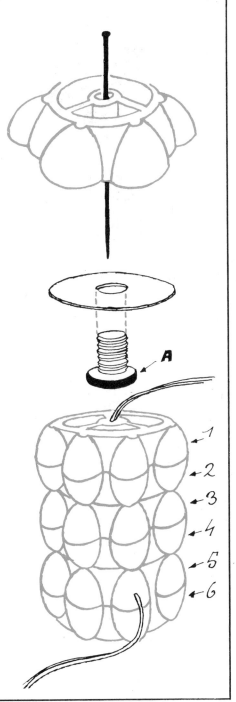

MATERIAL

- Three or four round cartons.
- Glue.
- Plaster and small stones.
- A large knitting needle.
- An equipped electric socket.
- A round piece of wood or metal, 2 inches in diameter and pierced in the center.
- A lamp shade corresponding to the height of the lamp.

PROCEDURE

- Pierce a hole in the center of the cartons with the knitting needle to allow for passage of the electric cord. Pierce tiers 1, 2, 3, 4 and 5 in this manner (see sketch opposite).
- To the top of the first carton, glue the round piece which has its center cut out to accomodate the socket (see sketch opposite).
- Pass the electrical cord through tiers 1 and 2. Screw on the socket. Glue the edges of the first carton together. Then pass the cord through the holes in tiers 3 and 4, glue the first and second cartons together, then glue the edges of tiers 3 and 4 together, and so on.
- Pierce a hole in the top half of the third carton (this is the exit-hole for the cord), and glue this carton to the one above it.
- Pour plaster into the bottom of the third carton (tier 6), and also add some small stones to weight the lamp and assure stability.
- Glue the edges of tiers 5 and 6 together. The lamp is complete.

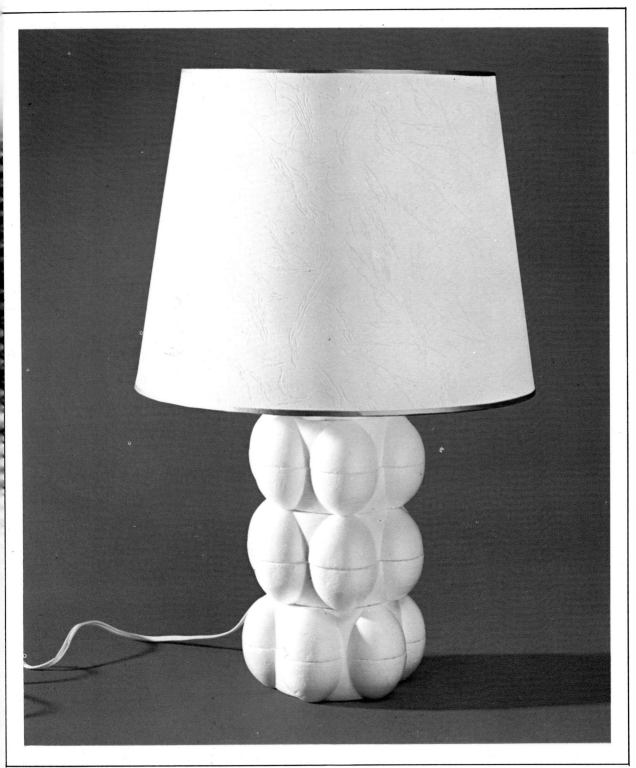

OTHER IDEAS

This attractive lamp can be modified according to your personal tastes; you can make it taller by increasing the number of cartons used. In this case, you should also weight the upper tiers with plaster and stones.

You can also simply add a half-carton on the top (tier 0), in which case you must cut away the notches of the central closure to allow for incorporation of the socket. The round piece which holds the screw foot must be 2 inches in diameter in order to fit into the central opening.

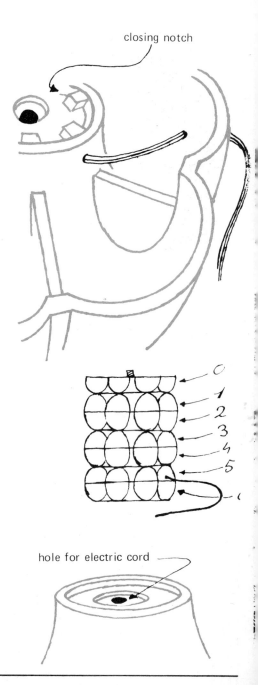

closing notch

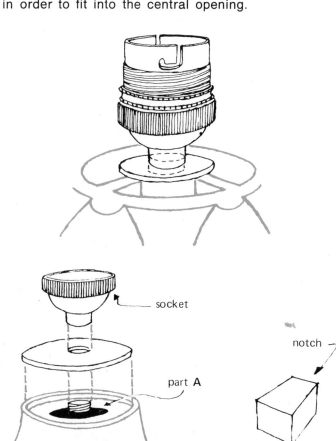

socket

part A

notch

hole for electric cord

DATE DUE